Standing In the Mid-Air of Faith

TimEtta Pipkins Wilson

Copyright 2010 TimEtta Pipkins Wilson. Printed and bound in the United States of America. All rights reserved. No part of this book may be reproduced in any form or by any means without prior written consent of the publisher, except in brief quotes used in reviews. For more information, write to the poet at timettayp@yahoo.com.

Publisher's Cataloging-in-Publication data

Wilson, TimEtta Pipkins.
    Standing in the mid-air of faith / TimEtta Pipkins Wilson.
    p. cm.
    ISBN 978-0-615-38067-4
1. Spiritual life --Christianity. 2. Christian life. 3. Conduct of life. 4. Families -- Religious life. 5. Christian women --Religious life. I. Title.

BV4527 .W559 2010
248.8/43--dc22   2010908746

Cover art by TimEtta Pipkins Wilson
Photo of author by Sherwin Johnson

Designed by RootSky Books,
www.rootskybooks.com.
RootSky Books is a division of RootSky Creative,
www.rootskycreative.com.

This book is dedicated to

My mother, Victoria Louise Tottress Pipkins, a strong woman of faith, ingenuity, intelligence, resilience and love. You are an exemplary mother who taught her children well.

And to
My father, Tim Allen Pipkins, Sr., who is now resting in his grave until Jesus comes. Daddy, you are the first man I loved and laughed with. I inherited your "jack-of-all-trades" abilities.

And to
My three wonderful children whom I love dearly.
You are:
Granville Oliver Edgar: Grand village of peace
Victor Richard Timothy: Mighty conqueror honoring God
Olivia Victoria Gwendolyn: Peaceful victorious warrior

Contents

Acknowledgements — i
Standing in the Mid-Air of Faith — iii
Introduction — vii
In the Beginning — xv

SECTION I
From My Heart to Yours

The Braided Cords of the Trinity — 2
From the Cradle to the Cross — 3
From the Garden to the Grave — 6
Nothing Less — 8
The Centipede Centurion — 9
The Beautiful Brown Cow — 10
Small Miracles — 12
What Do you Want from Me? — 13
All Alone — 14
A Quiet Song — 15
Help Me Remember Not to Forget — 17
Christmas is Over — 18
God's Valentine — 19
Letetia Ann Booth Boles — 20
For Baby Aston — 21
His Truth is Marching On — 23
Spoken — 25

SECTION II
Short Poems, Haiku, and the Like

From a Slave's Point of View — 32
Man — 32
Earth-Quakes — 32
Blooming — 33
To Be or Not... — 33
Someone's Missing — 34
Poem About a Poem — 35
Watch Out — 35

SECTION III
Healing Streams for the Soul (CD)

Worship in Majesty	38
Cause Me to Trust	39
Wind Beneath My Wings	41
So Little... So Much	42
Little Brown Sparrow	44
Sand Castles	45
Man of Sorrows	46
Dime Store Pearls	47
God's Valentine	48
It's Okay for a Man to Cry	49
Cacophony	50

SECTION IV
It's a Family Thang – *We all Write!*

Wise Words from Mama	54
Wadell the Traveler	55
Help Me See	56
Don't	57
Am I Beautiful Yet?	58
One Flesh	60
Wife-to-Be	61
Precipice	62
What Will I Do With Jesus?	63

SECTION V
Spiritual Spinach for the Soul   66

Acknowledgements

This book brings with it so much joy and love. Many people helped make me the person I am, and each of you contributed to helping me bring forward this project. It is here that I acknowledge your love.

Constance Elaine Sams Green (Connie), my sister in the Lord, who encouraged (made) me to do this project, thank you.

P.Rich, my friend, my reality check, my balance, you always give me words of encouragement and love. Thank you for believing in and praying for me.

R. L. S. Burse, who says I have enough brains for two people, I truly appreciate you.
Dr. Norwida Marshall, my counselor, advisor, friend to the end, your words mean so much to me.

Johnnie Mae Maberry, Charles Lindsey and Joslyn Davis, you are three outstanding artists and friends. Phillip and Rosalind Wooley, R. Kennedy Gates and Letetia Boles, thank you for being a part of my journey. And thank you Jennie Sturgis for all your help.

My family, who always have my back, I don't have enough words to express my deepest love and appreciation for you.

My beautiful mother, Victoria, you lovingly still keep everyone straight.

My terrific brothers whom I have always loved and admired: Tim Allen Pipkins (Jr.), Hume (deceased), Victor (deceased), Dwayne Lee Pipkins (and your lovely wife, Julia), Wadell Ray Pipkins (and your beautiful wife, Florence), I love you all.

I am so grateful to the following families for helping me become who I am today: Tottress, Williams, Nero, Pipkins, and Wilson.

Last but not least, to the most high God, my ADONAI, my husband, Lord and Master. Isaiah 54:5. You are my everything.

TimEtta Pipkins Wilson

Standing in the Mid-Air of Faith

Chorus

Have you ever stood in the mid-air of faith?
Have you ever trusted in His unchanging grace?

Have you looked so foolish when you said,
I simply trust Him!

Have you ever stood in the mid-air of faith?

Verse 1

Standing on His promise, believing in His Word,
Never doubting, always shouting,
Lord I need you now!
Acting out my faith by working in His holy will.

Have you ever stood in the mid-air of faith?

Verse 2

Oh, the mid-air of faith takes you up an awesome flight,
Standing on His word and then using it for sight,
All those precious promises they are for us to use,
Trust Him friend, oh trust Him,
In the mid-air of faith.

Verse 3

The mid air of faith my friend,
Is a very scary flight,
Not knowing where you'll end up,
On this journey here on earth,
Just trusting like dear Abraham, guided by His light.
Have you ever stood in the mid-air of faith?

Verse 4

Oh, the mid-air of faith my friend,
Tests your strength in Him,

Standing in the Mid-Air of Faith

We can hardly please Him,
Without stepping out in Faith.

Surrender all to Jesus and He'll help you by His Grace,
Just stand my friend, Just stand In the mid-air of faith!

Introduction

A Personal Perspective of Standing in the Mid-Air of Faith

What do I mean? Well just suppose you or I could stand in the middle of the beautiful clouds we see as we fly through the air in a jet plane. No parachute, just the air, having no super hero abilities like Superman. Of course this doesn't happen, except maybe when your faith is challenged or tested to take a risk.

Standing on the shore of Clear Water Beach in Bermuda, I watched the sun come up as God spoke to me. My thoughts had become prayers: My marriage was disintegrating. My career was presenting me with several options — should I stay at my teaching job in Bermuda or return to the States to a job awaiting me there? I was at a crossroads in my career. My three children needed to be encouraged.

I lived on the beautiful island of Bermuda from 1995 until 1998 with my Bermudan husband and three children. My husband and I taught at Bermuda Institute. I had left Chattanooga, Tennessee after 20 years for Bermuda, thinking the adventure would be good for our children and praying the change would give our marriage the boost it needed.

While living in the States I had been in education for more than 18 years and had worked in parochial and public education. Our oldest son Granville was entering his senior year of high school. Our second son Victor was entering ninth grade. Our daughter Olivia was entering second grade.

I did my best to be a good wife and mother. I taught school, then came home to take care of my family. I worked hard to keep our children in Christian school. I also did my part to help neighborhood families with their education by carpooling and picking up all the neighborhood children to take them to school.

I convinced my husband that I needed a break from full-time employment and that it would be cheaper to teach everyone at home. Little did I realize that God had a hand in all of this.

So our home school — Maranatha School of Academic Excellence — began in September 1994. My children often teased me about having such long names for everything. But I had a reason for the long name. Home school was not popular, and I wanted my children to be able to talk about their wonderful school with honesty. If someone were to ask them what school they attended, they could truthfully tell them.

I became a dynamic change agent for my family by training my children in every area I could think of. Their education was no longer just about books and the traditional learning model. They learned life skills such as how to cook and even work skills that could help them earn a good living as adults. My children were trained to make bread, (about 10 loaves per week). In fact, we got so good that we began selling it to our church school. Their father, who was very handy with tools and construction, introduced them to carpentry. We remodeled the kitchen and replaced our front door and its frame.

We would go into nature, since we had woods behind our house and have science lessons. They received a lesson in life sciences when our dog gave birth to puppies. Scripture lessons were very important and we all learned chapters from the Bible and dramatized them. And of course all the academics were included. We took a long field trip to Casa Grande, Arizona to visit my mother who was about to have surgery. The kids learned map skills, land and cloud formation, and even the different states we traveled through as we made our way across the country. These are just a few of the lessons I taught my children in our home school

Now that I was home with my children, this gave me the opportunity to rise early each morning and spend private time in my own praise and worship with God. He kept nudging me to read the story of Abraham from the Bible. But each time I opened the Bible to this passage, I would start and never get to finish. It seemed that I would turn on the radio or be at church hear a sermon or a lesson on the life of Abraham and Sarah. I finally took the nudging seriously and got into a serious study of Abraham, the "Friend of God," in January 1995. I was so fascinated at how he readily obeyed God and how he just got up and moved at the age of 75!

*"... Get thee out of thy country, and from thy kindred,
and from thy father's house,
unto a land that I will show thee;"*
Genesis 12:1

I kept feeling as if somehow this story was going to affect our family. I thought perhaps we needed to prepare to move, but where, when, and how? We had always prayed about moving out of the city to the country —was this now the time? Well, as I shared things with my husband he thought that I had really lost it! Home school and now this! So I said no more, but kept it in my heart and in my prayers. However, in the back of my mind I wanted to sell the furniture and begin to pack. I really had the *"Abraham syndrome"* bad.

This yearning to move stayed with me from January until May.

About the latter part of April a call came from my husband's sister concerning my mother-in-law's need to have surgery. Knowing how serious the surgery would be, we began to make plans for Oliver, my husband, to go to Bermuda. Later on that week his sister called again to say that there were job opportunities for teachers at Bermuda Institute, and that when Oliver came, he needed to check out the teaching positions.

His sister called back that same week to say Oliver and I both should apply for work there. The next day the educational superintendent for the Bermuda conference called us and invited both of us to come for an interview.

"We can't do that," my husband said. "We can't afford for both of us to go."

With only one salary, our family's finances would not allow such travel. But the decision for me to stay behind did not bring peace to our spirits. We debated the issue and prayed on it, wondering if his sister's words held any truth. *Should I also go to Bermuda?*

A credit card offer arrived in the mail. We applied and were approved! That was a strange occurrence for us and we saw it as a sign, as we had not received any credit cards before (or since). So with credit card in hand and tickets purchased, all five of us traveled to Bermuda.

I had been once when Granville was a tiny baby, so this was only my second time visiting my husband's place of birth.

•

The wonderful, fish hook shaped island of paradise that we could see at one time from the air was an exciting place to be. Oliver's family and the conference officials warmly welcomed us.

We had traveled to the island to be with Oliver's mother because of her surgery, but the doctors revised their opinion and decided she did not need to have the operation at that time. But perhaps this was God's way of starting us on our Abrahamic Journey.

We did not rush back to the States. Instead, we followed through on our idea to find jobs. We were both hired to teach in the K-12 school, with a student population of approximately 500, at Bermuda Institute.

Our next challenge was to find housing. We were told that this was very difficult and that there would not be many choices. Housing was from $1,000 for a one bedroom apartment to $3,000 per month for an executive style apartment with three small bedrooms.

We prayed and looked without much success.

"Things don't look good," my husband said.

"Well, God has not failed us yet," I said. I called upon my heavenly House Hunter, and rehearsed the story of the five daughters of Zelophehad in Deuteronomy who wanted to receive property when they went to the Land of Promise.

"Father, I know I am one of your daughters," I prayed. "I know you have property for us. Please rain down your blessings on our family."

•

The day before we were due to go back to Tennessee we were blessed to find an executive apartment with four bedrooms and two bathrooms with a garage for $1,600! This was a miracle and God showed me that He can handle anything. It was five times more than we paid for our home in Tennessee with an acre of land. But for Bermuda in the '90s, this was a steal.

"Praise God!" I exclaimed.

"Amen!" My husband chimed in.

We returned to Tennessee excited to begin our packing and return to Bermuda by August of 1995. Now I knew why God had been urging me to pack and prepare.

•

Living in Bermuda was an unusual, unique experience for a Catholic girl who was born in Tulsa, Oklahoma then moved to Huntsville, Alabama with her uncle and aunt to go to a Seventh-Day Adventist college. My mother and father and brothers often said, "That this girl is really something!"

I never really followed the norm so this was a dramatic change affecting everyone.

But to borrow the words of Dickens, "It was the best of times, and it was the worst of times." I was very thrilled that our three children were experiencing living on the island where their father was born. My sons Granville and Victor seemed to adapt quickly. They got mopeds and scooters and wore Bermuda shorts. All three of our children were born in the South and had southern drawls. So they began trying to pick up British accents so they could fit in. Olivia suffered the most at first because she was only about eight years old and had to get used to going to school, making new friends and constantly being teased about how she talked.

Me, I loved the water and the rocks in St. David's which was the parish at the end of the island. They called this "Behind God's Back" because they said it was so far away. Mind you now, the island was only 21 square miles long. Here, I became a reflective researcher as I observed the ways of the island and the many different cultures, attitudes and traditions. I had a special place called Emily's Bay where I could sit on the huge boulders and rocks and watch the cruise ships come in as they blew there loud organ-like fog horns. This was my place to do some of my best writing, study nature and talk with God. This tiny island was a little taste of heaven.

But as beautiful as it was, the island could not save my marriage.

"Whatever you do, you must not allow anyone or anything to rob you of your faith in yourself." — T. D. Jakes

By the third year in Bermuda I knew there would have to be some drastic changes. As I stood on the beach, I reflected on the night before. I had lain in bed with tears streaming down my face and had cried out to God. "Lord, I need help! Show me your way."

•

The next morning, I was awakened by a still, small voice. God whispered, "Come take a walk with Me."

I loved early morning walks just before dawn. Slipping out of bed so as not to wake up Oliver, I left a note, grabbed my Bible and journal and headed for Clear Water Beach. It was down near the old American Army base. As I strolled along the beach it was very early and still cool.

I walked the length of the shore, dodging the cold tidewaters. God began to minister to me through nature. He quietly spoke to me through His Word. He invited me to walk into the cold water. I didn't really want to but gradually I did. I felt so close to my Lord, Savior and Friend.

In gentle whispers, He began to tell me of His love and how circumstances were going to get harder and more difficult. I looked down at my feet in the beautiful, brilliant blue, clear, water and I could see and feel the sand and rocks moving under my feet. God explained to me that just as the sand was shifting under my feet things would be just as uncertain in my home. But I was not to run away from Him when times got hard, but to come closer to Him and go deeper in His warm love. This quiet, overwhelming experience was so awe-inspiring. I saw the sun begin to come up over the waters. God was smiling on me.

I had been praying about another job possibility in the States. We had received a mysterious call from our good friends, the Copelands, about the church school needing a principal in Tennessee. They urged me to send a resume' to the conference there. I thanked them and just shook my head knowing that I did not even want to think about it. I even laughed at them and put it out of my mind.

However, I did go ahead and send my resume', just to see what would happen. I had a phone interview with the superintendent, Mr. J. P. Willis.

"We have five positions," he said.

"I will go anywhere but Mississippi," I told him.

I never wanted to live in that state because of the horrible reputation it had during the Civil Rights era. Wouldn't you know it... that's exactly the ones that responded first!

That morning on the beach, I finally surrendered. I gave God everything: my marriage, my children and my future. I let go and stopped trying to fix things. Once I let go and turned it over to Jesus, His calming peace settled in around me.

I had spent three years in Bermuda and it was time to go! At the end of my third school year I put in for my return to the States (we were considered missionaries). My two sons were headed for Oakwood University (It was Oakwood College in the '90s), in Huntsville, Alabama. My daughter, Olivia and I were headed for Jackson, Mississippi. But we had to go back to Chattanooga, our point of origin, before we moved. And my husband, wanted to stay in Bermuda.

"Be ready to quickly change again and again. They keep moving the cheese."
— Who Moved My Cheese by Spencer Johnson

I began my experience as a competent scholar as I became the Principal/teacher for E. E. Rogers SDA Academy. This dual role was challenging, rewarding and exhausting. To make ends meet on a teacher's salary is often a gymnastic feat! My estranged husband and I were separated. He sent some support but not consistently.

We eventually divorced in March of 2000. This was heart-wrenching for me, after 25 years. As a Christian I thought this should never have happened to me. My children often teased me of trying to create "Hallmark card" moments for our family. But you know, I realized it takes a team, not just one. Being a *married single* is no fun. I did not like the idea of being on someone's statistic chart. This new situation of being in a strange place, a new position and now a divorce was a lot to handle. But drawing on God's strength and using my emotional intelligence to look introspectively at my situation, I reflected on my walk and talk on the beach in Bermuda.

" And {TimEtta} shall be like a tree planted by the rivers of water; Her leaf also
Shall not wither; and whatsoever {TimEtta} shall do shall prosper," Psalms 1:3

My mother, a powerhouse when it comes to getting things done, gently insisted that I record my poems. I often wrote poetry and used it for making my personal greeting cards. Once again I began implementing change in my own life. One night in December of 1998, I was feeling low. Christmas was coming and I didn't know how I was going to get presents. I put on one of my favorite instrumental CDs by Roland Gresham. Roland is a very talented gospel-jazz guitarist. Sitting in the middle of my bed, legs crossed, poetic phrases began to develop in my mind. It was as if God was letting me know through my own words that it was going to be all right. I grabbed a pen and paper and began to write down my words quickly to the music of "Wind Beneath My Wings."

I called Roland the next day and explained what I had done. After a long delay on my part (thinking my work wasn't good enough), I sent it to him. He loved it and said we should start recording as soon as possible.

We discussed and planned what I had in mind with the poetry and began to work. Step by step, in the studio that Roland used, we began recording. This was exciting! Jackson, Mississippi and Nashville, Tennessee are about 400 miles apart, so this was a slight drawback. However, I have learned that man's impossible situations present God with opportunities to create miracles.

I began recording in Headroom Studio in April of 2000. Roland composed and created inspirational music to fit my poetry reading on the spot. It was amazing!

"And Jabez was more honorable than his brethren: and his mother called his name Jabez, saying, Because I bare him with sorrow.
And Jabez called on the God of Israel saying,
Oh that thou wouldest bless me indeed and enlarge my coast, and that thine hand might be with me and that thou wouldest keep me from evil...And God granted him that which he requested."
I Chronicles 4:9,10

Penny by penny, and month by month, my project grew and developed. I learned about the Jabez prayer in I Chronicles 4:9,10, and began praying for God's hand to be on my poetry project and with me. In about six months the recording was finished. The project could have been finished sooner but because of the distance and finances it was slow going.

The Lord gave me the idea to do mail order promotions.

The next stage was the duplicating. I was very determined to complete this project, being the effective leader and public relations agent that I am. Still praying, and using whatever extra money God sent my way, I finally had enough to get the duplicating started. Exactly 30 days after beginning my Jabez prayer, on March of 2001 my "poetry baby" was born! The title: "Healing Streams for the Soul."

Just as God taught Moses how to use that old stick — that shepherd's rod — to cast before Pharaoh, open the Red Sea and even bring water from a rock, so God wants us to use the "stick" that is in our hand. I was a willing servant and chose to use my creative talent and voice to touch lives.

What about you? What talent, what skill do you have? Use it to His glory! God was showing me how to take what I had in my hand and glorify Him. In my case, my stick — my shepherd's rod — was this CD project. Through this experience I have seen my heavenly Father and Friend show me how to trust Him with all my heart, as it says in Proverbs 3:5, "Trust in the Lord with all thine heart; and lean not unto thine own understanding."

He [God] will bless you a hundredfold if He knows you will not worship what He gives you...
She maximizes her potentials but she doesn't worship her ambitions."
— T. D. Jakes The Lady, Her Lover, and Her Lord" p. 172,173

    No, I am not rich and famous in the world's eyes, but I am rich in the knowledge of seeing God answer my prayers specifically. I like to say that He tailor makes our answers to fit our specific needs and even the unspoken desires of our hearts. He really wants us to learn how to Stand in the Mid-Air of Faith, with absolutely nothing but HIM to hold on to!!

    The book you now hold in your hand is another example of a mid-air experience! I am walking by faith as I share my journey and pray my words can help you on your own way. The mid-air of faith is a place where we are suspended above our doubts as we reach for the manifestation of God's glory. May the blessings of my Heavenly Pilot be with you as you test your wings to stand in the mid-air of faith.

TimEtta Pipkins Wilson

In the Beginning

And God said, "I'm lonely."
I'll make Me a world,
And in this world I'll make me a little Girl.

And God looked and looked until He saw,
A man and wife,
Tim and Victoria Pipkins,
Way in Tulsa, Oklahoma,
And they begat — TimEtta.

I have made sure that she will be surrounded by
Strong brothers,
Two older — from a previous marriage,
Tim and Hume,
And three younger,
Victor, Dwayne, and Wadell.

But Victor the tender-eyed one, will be shamefully taken away,
At 17 in a car accident by a drunken driver,
But there still will be four.

Now God knew while she was in her mother's womb
According to Psalms 139:13-16
That He would...
Shape her before she was born;
"You put my bones together while I was still in my mother's womb,
I praise you for this body is incredibly and wonderfully made,
Your whole creation is a marvel and,
I know that it all didn't Just happen.
When I was developing in my mother's womb
Nothing took place that you didn't know.
To you there is nothing secret and mysterious."

God said, I want My little girl to be,
Unique, gifted, and blessed.
She will be creative, so He gave her the gifts of

Standing in the Mid-Air of Faith

Writing, painting, dancing, laughing and loving people.

Next, I will give her skills and abilities,
To teach, to lead, to administer and,
To bring order out of chaos.

Now my daughter will marry and,
Conceive three children by one man.
Granville III, handsome, reckless, godly,
Victor Richard, a child that will honor Me,
Olivia Victoria, the lily of the valley, a help to her mother,
Each one taught of the Lord.

God thought a little longer and decided,
She will need a tender heart,
A heart like Mine,
A bleeding heart... she will not like this but,
I will need her to reach others for Me,
And share the gospel around the world.
She will need to bind up the broken-hearted
And set the captives free.

Now, TimEtta is no longer a little girl.
She is...
The woman,
The Leader,
The Teacher,
The Dancer,
The Artist and poet,
The Evangelist.
A woman created in the image of God,
This is whom you see.

SECTION I

From My Heart to Yours

The Braided Cords of the Trinity

As strands of rope are braided,
So be the strands of love and prayer.

For *Love* takes hold of prayer,
Because remember, God is Love.

The incense of prayer wafts gently upward,
Wrapping around the legs of Love.

That sister that cries,
Behind closed doors,
Needs to feel the hug of *Prayer and Love.*

Or what about the wounded soul,
That just went through a devastating divorce,
Do his prayers go up in a puff of smoke?
Thinking that Love does not hear him.

But Love and Prayer are partners,
Working to bring about good,
You've heard that prayer changes things,
Well, it really, really does.

Allow *Love* to be the Master,
Lay your head on the breast of the Spirit,
Our most holy *Comforter,*
Sit in the Lap of the Father and rock,
Until you fall asleep.

As the braided cords of the Trinity,
Rock you in their arms,
Your prayers are already answered you see,
Before you utter your heartfelt plea.

TimEtta Pipkins Wilson

From the Cradle to the Cross

From the cradle to the cross,
Was it a loss?

For Mary's little baby,
To be born in swaddling clothes,
In a feeding trough.

Animal smells,
Straw and hay in a cave,
My Savior, Your Savior,
Born to die?

The Shadow of the cross always following Him.

As Mary rocked Him in her arms,
She wondered about harm,
 Would anyone believe,
He'd come to save the world?
This little infant so meek and so mild,
Mary's little baby?

The God of All!

Cutting His first tooth,
Changing dirty diapers…
Mama watches as He changes,
Crawling,
Now toddling,
Oh, how proud they were.
But the Shadow of the cross…still followed Him.

As a teen in the carpenter shop,
Handsome and strong,
I'm sure He must have had girls checking Him out.

Standing in the Mid-Air of Faith

But my Jesus, yes this Jesus,
Mary's teenage son,
Kept His eyes on the mission that He knew about.

As He baffled great scholars and Pharisees,
His knowledge of the scriptures stood way, way out.

Miracles at the wedding,
Changing water to wine,
Raising the dead, giving sight to the blind,
Making demons flee…
De-liberate-ly!

Calling the 12 that He would teach for 3 years,
Shedding many tears, because of their fears.

Looking over His shoulder still seeing that Shadow,
The shadow of the cross standing nearby.

He knew the time was very near,
The call came for Him to remain,
Just little while longer on this plane.

To give to the world,
His disciples,
His people,
One more lesson,
The one so hard to comprehend.

Not to be an earthly King,
But a lamb-like sacrifice.

The shadow of the cross,
Magnifying, terrifying, showing itself.

Now that Shadow,
That great Shadow of the
Dreadful cross,
Moves right in front,

TimEtta Pipkins Wilson

Face to face with the Savior Jesus Christ.

The cross, no more a Shadow,
Standing right there,
Looming and threatening in front of Him!
Salvation rings out with each deadly blow,
As the spikes spurt the blood,
Of our Savior meek and low,
From the cradle to the cross,
Not at all a loss!

From the Garden to the Grave

Written by request for the Johnson Family
In Loving Memory of Washington Johnson, Sr.

If only Adam and Eve knew,
The consequences one bite would do.

If only they could see as God saw,
That life and death was in the power of the jaw.

God warned them and taught them personally,
To trust Him and stay far away from that tree.

The serpent, the dragon, the arch enemy,
Induced and seduced the weaker of the two.

They ran and they hid when they heard God's voice,
Now realizing they had made the wrong choice.

The first lamb was slain by the lamb of God,
To clothe the couple that felt so odd.

To see their pet, have to shed its blood,
Oh, what a shame as their tears made a flood.

Centuries later we can still see the results,
That, that one act (of disobedience) caused for all adults.

Sin so powerful rears its ugly head,
Its partner is Death who stretches out instead,
Its sinister fingers,
To take the life of the righteous ones.

So noble, so regal, so kind, and mild,
Stood Washington Johnson father of six.

TimEtta Pipkins Wilson

If only he could have spoken to Adam and Eve,
To let them know what a legacy they would leave.

Janice and Cynthia, Stephanie and Rosalind,
Chosen women children of Eve.

Then Washington Jr, and Grayland too,
Would shake hands with Adam the father of you.

But alas, death has stolen this gentle man from the arms of,
His beloved Mildred, wife of many years.

From the garden to the grave, if only they knew,
What that one bite would cause and do.

But, we have a promise of victory,
That doesn't all end in misery.

God the Son will soon blow His trumpet so loud,
To let Washington Sr. know its time to get up!

Death will no longer be able to hold,
This saint, the soldier, this child of God.

He'll rise with the angels by his side,
With that charming smile,
He'll look around to see his dear family ascending with him.

Jesus the conductor of that heavenly train,
Will bring us to His garden once again.

But this time,
No sin,
No sadness,
No death,
In the garden of Gardens in heavenly bliss,
We'll spend time with Jesus for all eternity,
And sin and the grave will never be missed!

Nothing Less...

Your heart stands still when a loved one dies,
Will death ever lose its sting? ... you ask.

Your heart must be built on,
Nothing less,
Than Jesus' blood and righteousness.

The world keeps going at its frantic pace,
No one seems to notice that there's one less soul!
Your memories melt into reflective pools,
Of bygone years and days of old.

Let your hope be built on,
Nothing less,
Than Jesus blood and righteousness.

He's coming back to wipe away tears,
To destroy the sting and Death itself.

Build your hope on Him and,
Nothing else but His blood and righteousness.

He cares for you and desires to ease,
The grief and stabbing empty pain.

You must build your hope on Him right now,
And wholly lean on His dear name,
For Christ is your solid Rock today,
All other ground is sinking sand.
Let Him hold your sinking heart of sand,
And wholly lean in His dear arms.

TimEtta Pipkins Wilson

The Centipede Centurion

Century = 100 years
Centurion = Captain over 100 soldiers
Centipede = an insect with 100 legs and feet

About a century ago there was a **Centipede** who was a *centurion,*
Now the Centipede who was a centurion had a 100 centipedes under his command.

And the centipede Centurion had a problem,
Finding shoes for his 100 centipede soldiers,
Because that meant that he needed 10,000 shoes!

Sooo, the Centipede Centurion became creative,
And had 10 centipedes stacked on top of one another,
Which made 10 stacks of 10 centipedes.
This still equaled 100 centipedes.

Can you tell me how many shoes the Centurion Centipede needed now,
For his 10 stacks of centipede soldiers?

Standing in the Mid-Air of Faith

The Beautiful Brown Cow

There once was a beautiful brown cow, with big beautiful brown eyes,
Who loved her owner very much!
She gave the sweetest, creamiest milk of any cow for miles around.

However, the owner, a slick, fancy farmer,
Only took from the beautiful brown cow,
With the beautiful brown eyes,
That gave the sweet, creamy milk.

He only pretended to like his beautiful brown cow,
And gave her only small handfuls of his rich, sweet, heavenly, hay to eat.

Now mind you, the hay was the best around,
But the slick, fancy farmer gave just enough of his rich, sweet heavenly hay,
To keep the beautiful brown cow baited...
And make her think he really cared.

The beautiful brown cow, with the beautiful brown eyes,
Gave her sweet creamy milk,
Day after day.

But the slick, fancy farmer gave very little back.
He only took, and took,
Thinking that this cow,
Will surely give and give!

But alas, the beautiful brown cow,
With the beautiful brown eyes,
Began to get thinner, and thinner.

She would kick over the bucket with the sweet, creamy, milk,
Trying to get the slick fancy farmer's attention.

But the slick, fancy, farmer, did not care properly, For his beautiful brown cow.

So the beautiful brown cow,

TimEtta Pipkins Wilson

With the beautiful brown eyes,
That gave the sweet creamy milk,
Knew she would die if she did not run away!

So that night. She pushed open the barn door
And squeezed through the gate... (she was just that thin),
And ambled off so weak... To find someone who would feed her,
And not just take advantage of her, only for her sweet, creamy milk.
Well... the slick, fancy, farmer was stunned that his beautiful brown cow was nowhere to be found!
And by and by he realized,
Only too late,
That the beautiful brown cow,
With the beautiful brown eyes,
That gave the sweet creamy milk,
Was gone forever!

He wished now that he had given her more of the rich, fresh, heavenly hay,
And the kind and tender love she deserved,
Instead of taking advantage,
Of the beautiful brown cow,
With the beautiful brown eyes,
That gave the sweet, creamy milk.

So the moral of this story is:
When one gives from the heart, don't take advantage of them.
Know that it is a Christ-like love, of service, stronger than death. It is then not very wise to take it for granted or use it to ones own advantage. Because truly what one sows you will also reap. But if one does choose to give back, both will be rewarded with love, peace, and happiness.

Small Miracles

As I stretch forth my hand,
I reach for love,
Intangible though it may be.

There are many ways God let's us touch the unseen,
Just think my friend and you will see.

(Chorus)

The budding trees of a new-born spring,
The tender flight of butterflies,
The warming rays from the sun above,
God knows we need to feel His love,
God knows we need to feel His love.

God's heart is open to give you love,
He knows your every need,
He longs to hold you in His arms,
And give you eternity.

(Bridge)

So God sent His love,
His precious Son,
He sent His Son for us to touch and see.

(Back to Chorus)

Poem put to music and sung by Barry Richardson in Bermuda in 1997.

TimEtta Pipkins Wilson

What Do You Want from Me?

As I gaze at the people walking by I see...

People talking just to hear themselves talk...
Many words but nothing to say.

Empty expressions and empty dreams
Empty living day after day

***

Lord, What can I say to give them hope?
How can I help them see,
How do I show them Jesus love,
Lord, What do you want from me?

(Refrain)

Do I paint them a picture of your death on the cross?
Do I sing a melody of praise?
What will you have me do or say?
So all won't be in vain.

Jesus said,
Tell them I chose the way of a man,
I left my throne for Calvary,
Nobody knows how hard it was,
To leave my precious Father's side.

Do I paint them a picture of the golden streets?
Do I sing a melody of praise?
What will you have me do or say?
So all won't be in vain.

(Back to refrain)

Standing in the Mid-Air of Faith

All Alone

Sometimes I want to be all alone,
Yet close to my Savior's side.

Living in this world, makes me want to run and hide,
Yet I know I must go on.

Teardrops reflect little gleams of light,
Rainbow colors glisten from each drop.

I just want to stop — but...
I stop long enough to look up and see,
It's almost time.

It's almost time for the King to come,
And I won't be all alone,
For surely I'll be by his side,
And I won't have to run and hide,

Joyous tears will reflect the rainbow's light,
Around the great white throne.

It's almost time, its almost time,
It's almost time for King Jesus to come,
And we won't be all alone!

TimEtta Pipkins Wilson

A Quiet Song

Written by request for a Sickle Cell Fundraiser

Your Love is like a quiet song,
Heard only in the night.

When my pain and tears cry out,
You are there without a doubt.

Your love is like a quiet song,
Heard as I struggle and fight.

Trying to wrestle with this thing,
This sickle-shaped enemy.

But Your love is like a quiet song,
That soothes and raises me up.

I am but a child of yours,
Caught in the web of life.

My blood does not flow so well,
And it causes me nothing but strife.

Oh, but Your love is a quiet song,
As quiet as falling snow.

You rock me gently in your arms,
And keep me from all harm.

Your blood flowed so easily,
As you died on Calvary.

So I know you must understand,
My pain and agony.

Your love *is* my quiet song,

Standing in the Mid-Air of Faith

That you only sing to me.

To ease my hurting aching life,
As I learn to be so strong.

It's Your quiet song of tenderness,
That understands my grief.

You are the One, the only One,
That can give sickle cell relief.

You touch my veins,
And my pain takes flight.

Your love is like a quiet song,
That serenades me through the night.

Heard only in the night,
Heard only in the night.

TimEtta Pipkins Wilson

Help Me to Remember Not to Forget

I forgot about Your love and began to run away,
I forgot about our walk on the beach and did not reach.

Reach up for your hand, look down at Your love,
What's the matter with me when I forget who You are?

My tears blind my eyes,
My love tells me lies.

My tears keep me blocked,
My pain tears at my experience,
It has me locked.

How can I forget that You love me so much?

Immerse me in your love,
Baptize me with your Spirit.

Take my hand, take my heart,
Fortify me for a new start!

Standing in the Mid-Air of Faith

Christmas is Over

Christmas is over,
The shopping has come to a halt,
The gifts are received,
Some lie discarded,
Unappreciated,
Unwanted.

Where is the Christ-Child?

Lying in a manger,
A figurine in a nativity scene,
Under torn-up wrapping paper.

Christmas without the Christ the Messiah or the Universe?!

Where do we go when Christmas is over?

To Him, to the Babe
Who lived to die...

He's now the God-Man,
Divinely human, and always bearing,
The scars of His trek on earth,
Providing gifts for us.

When Christmas is all over,
Where do we go?

TimEtta Pipkins Wilson

God's Valentine

You gave to us your only Son,
Wrapped in a package of swaddling love,
Divinity clothed in humanity,
A heart of love sent from a dove.

A Valentine that is yours and mine,
Just ask and He will stay with you,
He said, "I will never, ever leave you!
I am here to stay right in your heart."

I love you dear one,
More than you know,
I died for you a long time ago,
I've got a mansion prepared for you,
With all kinds of gifts,
Just waiting for you.

Hold out your hand and close your eyes,
This little gift is just for you.

When I opened my eyes,
My Valentine had,
Placed a tiny heart of gold in my hand.

He said,
One day you will walk on streets of gold,
And know the piercing, aching, love so bold,
Of a crucified Lover,
Who cares for you.
Listen to me,
Don't ever doubt your destiny,
It's all wrapped in love for eternity.

Just trust me with your lonely heart,
I'll keep it safe,
Until we meet again,
In my blessed heavenly place.

Letetia Ann Booth Boles

For my sister in the Lord.
Happy birthday!

Sisters, sisters,
Bold in the Lord,
Under the Banner,
Washed in the Blood.

On the Battlefield,
Taking time out,
Enjoying, encouraging,
True Christian love.

Laughing and talking,
Whispering prayers,
Hearts wide open,
Filled with God's love.

We get so beat up,
Trying to open our hearts,
To reach out to others,
And mend the downtrodden,

As sister, sisters,
We have been blessed,
To have each other,
To call and reflect.

On our journey,
Through life and,
Then onward to Heaven,
We'll surely be sisters,
Sisters in Jesus,
Sisters by the Blood.

TimEtta Pipkins Wilson

For Baby Aston

Written by Request for a Baby Blessing

So tender and mild,
A boy, baby child.

Born of a woman,
Little Aston was born,
July 28, 2002,
Who even knew?

The angels in heaven knew,
And saw the God of all,
Mold and shape,
This little one,
Weighing only 5 pounds and 11 little ounces.

God witnessed the conception,
Of this tiny little human,
Who was made to reflect,
The image of God.

No, his parents aren't perfect,
But neither are we,
Just hold him, and love him,
That's what Jesus would do.

Mama and Daddy,
You're responsible too,

Pray over him, bless him,
Teach him right from wrong,
That is your duty, along with,
The church family.

Standing in the Mid-Air of Faith

You must raise,
Aston Da'von Myles,
To always serve God,
And don't forget your daughters,
Train them all to fear God.

For Jesus is coming soon,
And He's sure to ask you,
Where oh, where is your,
Wonderful little flock?

So prepare them and yourself,
To meet Him in the air,
And make totally sure,
You all will be there!

TimEtta Pipkins Wilson

His Truth is Marching On

Soldiers marching,
Soldiers fighting,
What's this war all about?

Man is at war with his own heart,
Wrestling with right and wrong.

Weapons of mass destruction,
Cries of hungry, scared children,
People's hearts failing them because of fear.

His truth is marching on,
Even though lies seem to prevail,
God's truth is marching on.

Hold fast Christian Soldiers,
Prepare for the front lines of battle,
For the battle is not to the swift,
But to those that will endure.

His truth is marching on,
Believe me it will prevail,
It has stood the test of time,
So fear not my child, fear not.

Terrorist, bombs, and killings,
Who is the real enemy?
Who is the true defender?
Will we ever know?
The enemy terrorists are Satan and Death,
They band together to cause,
Misery, heartache and pain.

But the Commander-in-Chief is Jesus,
See His banner raised so high!
See the lightning flash in His eyes!

Standing in the Mid-Air of Faith

See Him coming in the clouds of glory!
Riding His angelic white horse.

He won the war a long time ago,
Upon Calvary's bloody hill.

So let not your heart be troubled,
Chirstian soldier,
God's got your back,
Just remember who's really in charge!

Our Commander- in-Chief is Jesus,
The Almighty Admiral, God the Father,
And the Five-Star General is the Holy Ghost,
What an awesome trio indeed!

His truth is marching on,
His truth is marching on,
Hold on Christian soldier,
He's gonna make you stronger,
Hold on just a little while longer!

TimEtta Pipkins Wilson

Spoken

God stepped out in space,
And He spat and He spoke,
And He molded and folded,
As He toiled without foil,
Until, a planet was born,
And He said,
It's all good!

Light and night, evening and morning,
Atmospheric, anatomy, hydrogen and oxygen,
Chemical compressions, explosions and implosions,
Unite in one harmonic voice,
To bring into being this universe unrehearsed,
And God said,
It's all good!

He flung stars and planets,
From his hips and fingertips,
Set up solar and lunar orbits,
Oh, what a trip!

Words became worlds,
Creatures became features,
Microscopic molecules unseen by human eye,
God spat and he spoke and said,
Its all good!

With the eye of an artist,
The word made flesh,
Steps back to admire,
What was once empty mire,
Now leading all to desire,
This heavenly place,
He knew it was — all good!

Standing in the Mid-Air of Faith

As He saunters and surveys,
As He walked and He thought,
Hummmmmmmm...
There's one thing missing,
I know what it is!!!!

He knelt by the crystal river,
The river of life,
God dug and he tugged,
Didn't even use a knife,
Until he brought forth,
Lumps of glistening brown clay,
No haste or waste — did it without delay.

This time he decided,
I will not speak or spit,
I will mold and hold,
This being I'll call — man.

So god kneaded and pleaded,
And smote and smoothed,
Formed and fashioned,
This muscular, masterpiece, this being to behold.

As he consults the Godhead,
Three in one they are,
Father, Son and Holy Ghost — Elohim,
So esteemed!
Creator god says, "Let's make him in our image,"
Yes, they say, "After our likeness,"
So they all agree,
To set the clay free!

With a mighty blast,
From nostril to nostril,
From tongue to lungs,
From no heart to heartbeat,
The breath of life that will last and last,
Brings forth the man.

TimEtta Pipkins Wilson

Adam — a living breathing soul,
And Elohim said together,
Now, that's all good!

The mate they create,
To help procreate,
Fine, fabulous, female,
From one of Adam's ribs,
Two become one,
Oh, what fun!

Until some time later,
Unfortunately, there's a fall,
Someone dropped the ball,
But that's not all!

Centuries later, my creator,
Of the earthly theater,
Became a tiny seed,
Because there was a need,
To implant himself like a surgeon,
Into a young virgin.

And the spoken word became flesh,
So that he could pass the test,
That the first Adam — messed up,
Made the devil — shut up,
And God the father said,
It's all good!

And now my friend,
We're coming to an end,
Men are corrupt,
Everyone's wondering — "What's up?"
Jesus is coming back,
People having heart attacks.

It ain't all good,
If only they would,

Standing in the Mid-Air of Faith

Turn to the father,
And not bother to holler,
Always trying to make a dollar.

They would soon know,
And Jesus would show,
He is the way, the truth, and the light,
Uh oh, it's a dark night.

God stepped out in space,
And he spake and he spat,
He burned and he churned,
Ended sin right then.

Breathed new life in place of strife,
Turned sinners into saints,
A new heaven, a new earth.

We look up, we look out,
The new Jerusalem, we all shout!
Coming down like a crown,
God looks around,
And he says,
"It's all good,
Once again!"

SECTION II

Short Poems, Haiku, and the Like

From a Slave's Point of View

(I saw this picture in the home of Mrs. Ada Stigall)

Lil' Miss White Lillie Ann,
Sittin' at her pi'anna,
Whil'se I'se out here working' in da fields,
All fancied up in her,
Doll-like dress,
Whil'se I'se out here workin' in da fields.

•

Man

The physique of Man —
So powerfully sculptured,
So brilliantly sinued,
So marvelously computerized.

If breath was simply taken away —
Disalarmingly helpless,
Utterly lifeless,
Leaving nothing,
But molecules of dust!

•

Earth-Quakes *(haiku)*

The Earth swells, quivers, quakes
Silently opens, swallows houses, peoples, cities:
No one left to tell!

TimEtta Pipkins Wilson

Blooming (haiku)

Cherry blossoms open *g e n t l y,*
Cherry blossoms, man and woman, smell of love,
Fragrant scents of romantic love!

•

To Be or Not...

This is the age of the HIV,
To be or not to be.

This is the time to party hardy,
To be or not to be.

The rock, the smack, the coke, the stuff,
To be or not to be.

Abortion distortion,
Political corruption,
Forgetting the consequences until it's too late.
Nuclear warfare,
New World Order,
The next generation's gonna foot the bill.

To be or not to be... *That* is the Question!

Someone's Missing

(A tribute to Elaine — a co-teacher, Elaine Goodwin. Her car slid off a snowy mountain in Chattanooga, in 1984)

Life,
Goes on as if nothing happened!
The hustle,
The bustle,
The shuffle,
The pace.

Has no one noticed, A precious flower is missing;
One of God's own,
I'm sure He's noticed!
The hustle,
The bustle,
The shuffle,
The race.

Please,
Just stop one moment, touch someone near,
Just a kind word, a smile or a nod.
Listen world, someone is gone !

But the pace goes on, the race is on,
We pause briefly at life, taking it for granted…
Until it's gone,
The hustle,
The bustle,
The shuffle,
The waste!

Poem About a Poem

Poems are free-flowing measured thought...

Thoughts put down in rhyme and reason,
Thoughts with rhythm and with season,

Poems add savor to word flavor,
Make some sit up and take note.

So if you want to say it different,
Poetic form is the antidote.

•

Watch Out

Look out,
Look in,
Look up,
The Lord is about to come !

Look Out,
Look in,
Look up,
What are you going to do?

Look out for sin, it'll do you in,
Look in your soul, and take a poll,
Look up to heaven, and not at the reverend.

Look Out!
Look In !
And...
Look Up!

SECTION III

Healing Streams for the Soul

Standing in the Mid-Air of Faith

Worship in Majesty

Sun-kissed child of the Mighty One,
Let me teach you how worship is done,
Learn to worship Me as the sea,
Lift up your hands and praise only Me.

Cloud and sea majesty,
Speak to each other in intensity,
Ocean spray blown by the wind,
Kiss the clouds as they bow and bend.

White foam spray,
Whispy clouds array,
Their secret of how nature can pray.

Praise is seen in the clash of the spray,
As it leaps over rugged rocks without delay,
Teaching how to overcome strife,
As I lead you through this life.

Praise me when the trials come,
Don't fear, the battle's already won.

Learn to worship as the sea,
With freedom you can come to me.

Lie prostrate at my feet,
I will understand if you weep.

Learn to worship Me as does the sea,
To dance and leap beyond degree.
Learn to worship Me as the sea,
Sun-kissed child of my memory.

Learn to worship only Me,
Learn to worship as the sea.

TimEtta Pipkins Wilson

Cause Me to Trust

(A love letter from Jesus)

Last night I lay awake looking at the ceiling tears forming at the corners of my eyes,
Cascading gently down —
I'm tired dear Lord and I don't know what to do.

I don't know where you want me to go as your humble servant,
With that I closed my eyes and drifted off to sleep…

Awakened very early the next morning… Jesus said to me in a still, small voice,
I want you to work for Me,
Come take a walk with Me.

(I walked down to Clear Water Beach in Bermuda)
I walked along the edge of the tide,
Not wanting my feet to get wet,
Then my lord said to me,
"Step in the water and let your feet get wet."

I walked into the very cool water of the sea,
"This is my love. You first walked on the periphery of my love, now you are on the inside, and I am surrounding you."

Look down in the water you can feel the sand, Shifting under your feet, these are the unsure circumstances happening in your life.
But walk a little deeper into the morning tide and watch and see how the water holds you up and surrounds you. This is my love for you.

(As I walked deeper into the sea, God said…)
Don't walk on the edge of my love, for then I can't hold you up,
Immerse yourself in my love and though the earth around you is like the shifting sand under your feet,
My love is strong enough to well nigh hold you up.
The deeper you walk in the sea, the deeper your love for me.
This like faith, even though you can't see why, my love for you still,
Stands and surrounds you,

Standing in the Mid-Air of Faith

Trust me TimEtta.

When circumstances get hard, go deeper in my love.
Don't run away from me, but go deeper.
Love and faith go together,
You love me without seeing me,
You trust me and depend on me.
Love and faith go hand-in-hand.
Good people like Debbie and Larry show you real love. These people are genuine.

(As the sun begins to rise)

The sun shines on your face to let you feel my brilliance, warmth and everlasting love.
Remember these lesson i have taught you.
1. Walk on the inside of my love, not on the periphery.
2. Faith and love are the same.
3. There are good people that are genuine and will share my love with you.
4. I will always love you TimEtta. Understand my love and experience my love.

(I almost fell completely into the ocean with my clothes on)
If you fall for me you will not go wrong.
(A private joke between me and the Lord)

Remember the sea is salty and this is a symbol of my tears and love,
One day they will be tears of joy.

Psalms 84:11
For the lord god is a sun and shield: the lord will give grace and glory:
No good thing will he withhold from them that walk uprightly.

TimEtta Pipkins Wilson

Wind Beneath My Wings

Jesus is the wind beneath my wings,
He holds me up,
I glide like an eagle,
Because He is my wind.

Jesus blows gently and sends strong gusts,
I glide,
I ride,
I sail high,
He is my wind,
He is my strong current.

The wind beneath my wings,
That's who Jesus is.

No one knows how I keep flying,
It's only because of the wind,
He hold me up,
Blow strong wind,
Keep me steady, keep me sailing.

When the storm comes and the wind is oh so strong,
I will spread my wings and he will carry me even higher.

The stormy winds of the enemy blast and fight against my wings,
But the battle is not to the swift,
But to those that endure.

As the eagle, I set my sights on the higher purpose that beckons,
And spread my wings and fly.

Because Jesus is my steady,
Wind beneath my wings.

Standing in the Mid-Air of Faith

So Little... So Much

A towel,
Some sandals,
A bit of mud,
A braided cord...
Little things that did so much,
When Jesus picked them up.

He took the towel and washed their feet,
As all twelve looked with shock and disbelief,
Tenderly, pitifully, he looked at them all,
To be great, you must be small.
So little... so much.

And what about those sandaled feet:
Walking dusty trails only to find the need to
Heal the sick and raise the dead,
Arriving at Simon's house to dine,
No one to attend those precious holy feet,
Except for Mary's special treat.

So much... with so little.

He walked right by the blind beggar,
Until he heard, son of David, help me to see.
He spat in the dirt and made some muddy clay,
And told him go wash without delay.
As he washed his eyes he began to view,
The kind-faced sightgiver who now he knew.

Little is much...

The braided cord raised above his head,
Lightning flashing through his eyes,
All trembling, wishing to be dead,
As he clears the temple of all the lies,

TimEtta Pipkins Wilson

My house is a house of prayer!

And silently the children, the poor and the lame,
All that belong in the house of prayer,
Come sit by his side, and in his lap,
Clinging to every morsel of spoken bread,
Jesus, Yahweh, the great I am.
Takes little and makes so much… !

Standing in the Mid-Air of Faith

Little Brown Sparrow

This is the story of the little brown sparrow,
That sits atop an arrow,
You know one of those weather vane things,
Singing its quiet song.

I know the Master cares,
I know the Master dares,
Give me this little quiet song.

I sing because I'm happy,
I sing because I'm free,
I know my Master watches over me,
As I praise him from the tree.

My beauty's not seen on the outside,
It's what's on the inside that counts,
Simple faith and trust in the Master,
Is all that should be paramount.

I'll just sing my quiet little song,
That the Master gave to me,
I sing because I'm happy,
I sing because I'm free,
I know my Master watches over me.

Now, I'm just a little brown sparrow,
And the Master takes note of me on this arrow,
What makes you think that He's forgotten you?
You're certainly not out of His view.

Just sing this quiet little song my friend,
Then I think you'll see,
That his eye is not just on me you see,
But He's watching over you, too.

TimEtta Pipkins Wilson

Sand Castles

Have you ever built a sand castle...
Just a little too close to the tide?

Just as you get your towers just right,
And the drawbridge fixed upright,
You notice the water coming too close,
But you're busy constructing your fort,

O well, you say... my house is built firm,
My castle is gonna stand,
Even without support.

But as each hour passes, the tide moves in,
Slowly, steadily and then swallows,
The little castle of sand.

O my castle of sand,
My house built by hand,
I put so much labor into my castle of sand.

But my house was built on shifting sand,
And not on a firm foundation by the Master's hand.

Matthew 7:24-27 says,
A wise man built his house upon the rock...
The foolish man built his house upon the sand...
Which one are you?
On the sand or in his hand?

Standing in the Mid-Air of Faith

Man of Sorrows

Sometimes you wonder...
Does anyone care?
Is God really there?
Is anyone listening?

Emotions churn deep in the soul...
Does anyone care?
Can anyone feel...
The heartache, the longings for someone,
Somewhere — to reach out and touch,
To reach out and share.

Just a gentle embrace...
Does anyone care?
Is God really there?
"Yes, my child I care,"
Comes a gentle, but
Powerful reply.

I feel your longings,
Your heartaches,
Your sorrows,
Your cares.

Just lay them at my feet!
Take my yoke, it's lighter!
I know the depths of your innermost soul.

For you see...
I am the man of sorrows,
Acquainted with grief!
Yes, I care...

TimEtta Pipkins Wilson

Dime Store Pearls

We cling tenaciously to the dime store pearls,
Thinking that we have so much.

When God is ready to give to us,
The pearl of great price.

We hold on tightly not wanting to let go,
Thinking that God is going to steal them away.
When all he wants is to replace them my friend with,
Treasures greater than gold.

God's Valentine

You gave to us your only son,
Wrapped in a package of swaddling love,
Divinity clothed in humanity,
A heart of love sent from above.

A valentine that is yours and mine,
Just ask and he will stay with you,
He said, "I will never, ever leave you!
I am here to stay right in your heart."

I love you dear one,
More than you know,
I died for you a long time ago,
I've got a mansion prepared for you,
With all kinds of gifts,
Just waiting for you,

Hold out your hand and close your eyes,
This little gift is just for you.

When I opened my eyes,
My valentine had,
Placed a tiny heart of gold in my hand.
He said, "One day you will walk on streets of gold,
And know the piercing, aching, love, so bold,
Of a crucified lover,
That cares for you."

Listen to me,
Don't ever doubt your destiny,
It's all wrapped in love for eternity.

Just trust me with your lonely heart,
I'll keep it safe,
Until we meet again,
In my blessed heavenly place.

TimEtta Pipkins Wilson

It's Okay for a Man to Cry

It's okay for a man to cry,
Remember Jesus did for his friend Lazarus.

It's okay for a may to cry,
Remember Jesus did for Jerusalem.

Its okay to cry, strong men,
For tears are the cleansing of the soul.

Yes, crying hurts, but then it soothes,
As the comforter transforms and,
Translates your tears into prayers.

It's okay because the great I am,
Can touch the soreness of your soul,
And heal the brokenness of your heart.

It's okay to cry strong men,
For Jesus will fortify your spirit,
And build up your tattered image,
For you are His... made in his image,
He too lived as a man,
So he knows what you're going through.

Disappointments and unfulfilled dreams,
May slap you in the face,
Why shouldn't you cry?
For tears certainly cleanse and restore.

It's okay to cry strong men,
Because afterwards you can get back up,
And dry your eyes, square your shoulders,
And know for sure you're in the Master's hand.

It's okay to cry,
Remember,
Jesus did,
And he will make it right.

Cacophony

The violin sat in the corner of the room,
Dust-covered tunes,
No one's melody to assume.

Broken strings,
Broken dreams,
No one cares so it seems.

As each passing year rolls by and by,
No sound of music pierces the sky.

Suffocated by tragedy,
Melodies strain to escape morbidity.

Suddenly, the master musician,
Reaches out to touch,
This old violin no one thought was very much.

He replaced the strings,
Of broken dreams,
He blew off the dust to give,
Life a new theme.

He breathed music back,
Into the tuneless thing,
That so many though was worth nothing.

Music sang volumes as it,
Spilled forth from the bow,
Of the violin that looked so low.

As the conductor tapped his baton,
The orchestra sat oh so very alert,
To receive directions for his wand.

What's this I see?

TimEtta Pipkins Wilson

It's that same violin!
In musical majesty ready to perform,
Leaning gently on the Master's arm!

Knowing the notes, hearing the tunes,
As they crescendo loud and strong,
Listening as each note seems to say.

No more broken hopes,
No more shattered dreams,
I will only play what the Master deems.

My notes will be clear,
No more to fear.

For my music will be sharp,
And as gentle as a harp.

I'm no longer in the corner,
I'm not a mourner.

I will sing my violin notes,
With new grander hopes.

Finally, the Master places me,
Under his chin,
To reassure me we're gonna win.

***

Melodious phrases of love begin,
As he sways and bends with each,
Notes from above,
How will it end?

SECTION IV

It's a Family Thang —
We All Write!

Wise Words from Mama

The family that prays together will find time to do other things together. They talk, sing or write to express their thoughts. I've always encouraged my own children to make cards for birthdays or whatever the occasion might be thus giving them time to think and show their appreciation toward others. It also lets the recipient know how they feel.

We strive for perfection, creating an atmosphere to be or do our best. Since none of us is perfect, we do the best we can to get as close to perfection as possible...be all that we can be. If we do that we should feel a lot of gratification and satisfaction with ourselves.

Compliment and encourage others as well. A compliment goes much farther than a complaint...try it sometimes.

Everything depends on how we live our lives in this imperfect world. It is so important that we keep our lives on Who is in control, Who has the knowledge and wisdom as well as the understanding of everything. That's where our faith enters the picture. God is the only perfect being.

So if we look to that higher power everything will always end perfectly.

— Victoria Tottress Pipkins

TimEtta Pipkins Wilson

Wadell the Traveler

(My baby brother)

Truck driving is my life,
I don't much get to see my wife,
I know God's got my back,
And I don't really lack,
Cause it says,
In Proverbs Chapter 3 to:
"Trust in the Lord with all my heart and
Lean not unto thy own understanding,
In all thy ways acknowledge Him and He will direct thy paths."
That's why I don't fret,
And realize He's got it all set!

— Wadell Ray Pipkins

Help me See

Black men where ya been?
Taken from your land, sold into slavery,
Shackles on your feet,
Working' for master,
Hopin' for something' to eat,
Families are split, life is hard, being beat and whipped,
It makes you want to quit,
But it's by the grace of God we do persevere,
and we live on year by year.

Black men where ya goin?
Gonna be free,
The way God meant for me to be,
No more shackles on my feet,
I'll get myself something to eat,
Make my house into a home,
Have a family so I won't be alone,
Go to school, and get a job.
I'm free to be, what I want to be.

So Black men where are you?
With your families and at home,
In the office, hard at work,
In the church and at school,
But don't you be fooled,
Brothers are killing brothers, drugs are in our veins,
Prison cells are full, and jobs are hard to find,
Houses are not homes and mothers are left alone.

Are there shackles on my feet?
I'm hungry, how will I eat,
God meant for me to be free,
Oh Lord help me see.

— Dwayne Lee Pipkins (My brother)

TimEtta Pipkins Wilson

Don't

Don't whisper sweet nothings in my ear,
Because I have a father that knows all lies,
Don't tell me "I love you,"
Cuz I have a Father that will make you commit,
Don't say I'm beautiful unless you truly do,
Don't tell me you've been there when you haven't come close,
Because my father will make you believe your lies,
Don't say, "I'll never leave you,"
When you plan to do a one-night stand,
Don't say, "I'll never hurt you,"
When you plan to take away everything I hold dear,
Cuz what you give to me and others my father will return,
You want to know who's my Father,
My Father is God, Jesus is my brother, and Holy Spirit is my Comforter,
So don't mess with me unless you want to deal with my Father.

— Olivia V. G. Wilson (My baby girl)

Standing in the Mid-Air of Faith

Am I Beautiful Yet?

You're the one that said I was worthless,
For a second I believed you,
Had me doubting my abilities to be great,
And you didn't even have to open your mouth to say it,
Your actions toward me spoke loud and clear,
You never truly showed me how I was to love or receive love,
You just kept me in your hold,
Even helped me be depressed and miserable like you,
Just cuz you couldn't stand to see me grow,
Had me longing to be beautiful,
Cuz you never said I was,
But that was back in the day,
When you meant something to me now,
Hug now I could care less,
Sometimes I forget that you're even alive,
Now you're barely a memory,
And to think I called you daddy when,
You never even be came my father,
Just some guy that happen to marry my mother,
And donate the sperm that created my twisted soul,
So I got something to ask you,
Why did you start communicating with me,
When I gave up on you ever loving me,
Why did you ignore my longing to connect with you,
Why did I cry at the things said,
Why did it take me almost killin myself,
For you to say you'd be there for me,
And one last thing... am I beautiful to you yet...
Or do you just secretly hate my life... I always felt you did,
Not sure what to call you or to say wut you are,
Cuz you never been my father,
Don't know why I called you daddy,
When the only thing I truly ever got from you,
Was depression,
So tell me when did you start loving me,
Tell me... am I beautiful yet,

TimEtta Pipkins Wilson

Or do I need to go back and try again,
Maybe I will, let me try to be reborn through,
My mother and be recreated in the womb,
Just like that's impossible,
It's impossible to regain a relationship that you threw out the window,
You know what,
I am beautiful now! I see what I can be,
I've got it off my chest,
And God shows me I'm no less.

— Olivia Victoria Gwendolyn Wilson

One Flesh

By Devonnett S. Wilson (my daughter in law, Victor's wife)
(To my Husband)

And the two shall become one flesh,
Familiar words taken figuratively:
A divine allegory of an intricate blending,
Of two minds, two hearts, two beings,
In the mystery of matrimony,
How that two should become one,
Then another being...

A composition of the two now one,
Another mathematical complexity,
Of the one from two,
Is set in motion by the creator,
Through the inner workings,
Of a process — conception.

The two have become one flesh,
Literally, physically, in reality,
Our daughter is you and me,
The mystery of matrimony,
Brought to fruition,
The visible form of our invisible union,
Look at what our love has made!

See her, touch her, hold her,
She is us — one flesh from the two,
She is us, me and you,
Beautiful, irreversible,
Little piece of heaven,
Carved right from our hearts,
See her, touch her, hold her,
She is us,
And the two shall become,
One flesh.

TimEtta Pipkins Wilson

Wife-to-Be

*By Victor R. T. Wilson (My second-born son)
Written April 9, 2002 for my then fiancée/now wife on her birthday.*

My dear wife-to-be,
You have a beauty,
Of which I find it hard to write…

Is it like a flower,
Whose beauty is natural?
Is it like a rose,
The lover's gold,
Whose inner quality is life?
A virtue personified,
Materialized,
So the hand can hold?
I believe it is…

For your outer beauty,
Is a lovely reflection,
Of character being molded within,
With love,
Your husband-to-be.

Precipice

Standing on the edge I perspire,
Seeking to escape the tumultuous fire,
The desire within me is a part of reality,
Yet I know in my mind it's not enough to save me.

Standing alone on this ever-present precipice, I seek council,
Then I stop and review my past consciousness,
Times that I'd had to make the decision,
But I pushed them aside and now I keep wishing,
I had heeded the call, avoided the fall,
I understand now He would have given His all.

Scientific knowledge cannot rescue the least of us,
Get on your knees now and escape to fiery precipice.

— Granville O. E. Wilson, III Granville (My oldest son)

TimEtta Pipkins Wilson

What Will I Do With Jesus?

I see my surroundings,
They seem to be clear,
The first question I ask is,
"Why am I here?"

I look left, I look right,
I run forward to fight, my heart pounds,
My thoughts rebound — Maybe I search,
For that which I cannot have.

I look in the mirror and start to laugh,
The laughter haunts me, taunts me,
I want to escape, my tears trickle down on the inside,
Not my face.

I cannot comprehend the love Christ has for me,
Put aside all other questions, stop all the ruckus,
The first question I must answer is...
What will I do with Jesus?

— Granville O. E. Wilson III

SECTION V

Spiritual Spinach for the Soul

Standing in the Mid-Air of Faith

Spiritual Spinach for the Soul

(Better than Popeye's Spinach)

Whenever I was in Bermuda or somewhere not familiar and got homesick or very challenged with circumstances, I would pull out one of these quotes and read them over and over. They reminded me of the cartoon Popeye. When one of the villains would attack him he would pull out a large can of spinach to get extra strength. The quotations that follow are just a few of my Spiritual Spinach leaves. Use them to give you the extra strength you need to get through your day.

Isaiah 54:5,6 Living Bible
For your Creator will be your Husband.
The Lord almighty is His name,
He is your Redeemer, the Holy One of Israel,
The God of all the earth.
For the Lord has called you back from your grief —
A young wife abandoned by her husband…

I Corinthians 15: 58
Therefore my beloved brethren be ye steadfast, unmovable,
Always abounding in the work of the Lord.
For as much as ye know that your labor is not in vain in the Lord.

Testimonies to the Church Volume 8 p.177
He understands all about the situation in which we are placed,
And He will work in our behalf.
He is honored when we trust in Him,
Bringing to Him all our perplexities.
As we acknowledge before God our appreciation of Christ's
Merits, fragrance is given to our intercessions.
— Ellen G. White

Testimonies Volume 8 p. 10,11
In the darkest days, when appearances seem so forbidding, fear not.

TimEtta Pipkins Wilson

Have faith in God. He is working out His will, doing all things well
In behalf of His people. The strength of those who love and serve Him will be
Renewed day by day. His understanding will be placed at their service, that they may
Not err in the carrying out of His purpose.
— Ellen G. White

Lamentations 3:22-24
Through the Lord's mercies we are not consumed.
Because His compassions fail not,
They are new every morning,
Great is thy faithfulness,
The Lord is thy faithfulness,
The Lord is my portion says my soul, therefore I hope in Him!

II Corinthians 12: 9, 10
My grace is sufficient for thee,
For My strength is made perfect in weakness. Most gladly
Therefore will I rather glory in my infirmities, that the power
Of Christ may rest upon me.

Clear Word Bible
My grace is all you need. My power is seen best through people who have limitations. Your handicap will make you depend on Me, and that's when you'll be the strongest.

Our Father Cares (devotional) p. 148
Never for a moment should we allow Satan to think that his power to distress and annoy is greater than the power of Christ to uphold and strengthen... Every sincere prayer that is offered is mingled with the efficacy of Christ's blood. If the answer is deferred it is because God desires us to show a holy boldness in claiming the pledged word of God. He is faithful who hath promised. He will never forsake the soul who is wholly surrendered to Him.

For Speaking Engagements or to order:
Adonai 7 Ministries, Inc.
ADDRESS: P. O. Box 2604, Ridgeland, MS 39158-2604
EMAIL: timettayp@yahoo.com
WEBSITE: www.adonai7ministries.com

www.ingramcontent.com/pod-product-compliance
Lightning Source LLC
Chambersburg PA
CBHW080252170426
43192CB00014BA/2656